VOLCANOES AND EARTHQUAKES

Patricia Lauber

SCHOLASTIC INC.
New York Toronto London Auckland Sydney

PHOTO CREDITS

COVER: Earthquake, Oga Japan, by H. Yamaguchi/
Gamma-Liaison; Kilauea Volcano, Hawaii, by Ken Sa-
kamoto/Black Star.

Frontis, Vince Streano; pp. 2, 14, 17, 19 (bottom), 46,
48, 53, U.S. Geological Survey; p. 3, Judith Carlson/San
Francisco Examiner; pp. 4, 19 (top), 27, UPI; pp. 6, 21,
50, 54, 56, 63, AP/Wide World; p. 9, National Park Ser-
vice; p. 13, H.C. White Co./California Historical Society, San Francisco; pp. 34, 35, Italian Government
Travel Office; p. 39, Library of Congress; p. 41, Tad
Nichols/Photo Trends Inc.; p. 44, Consulate General of
Iceland; p. 62, The State Historical Society of Missouri;
p. 71, Randall Hyman; p. 72, Ralph Perry/Black Star; p.
75, David Falconer.

ISBN 0-590-32575-2

Copyright © 1985 by Patricia Lauber. All rights reserved. Published
by Scholastic Inc.

12 11 10 9 8 7 6 5 4   7 8 9/8 0/9

Printed in the U.S.A.   28

CONTENTS

When Mount St. Helens, in southern Washington State, began to stir, geologists were present to observe it and monitored it with instruments.

A Mountain Explodes

Like a giant waking from a deep sleep, the volcano named Mount St. Helens began to stir in mid-March 1980. From time to time the whole mountain shuddered. In late March it made a loud noise and then began to blow out steam, gas, and ash. A plume of steam billowed thousands of feet above its peak. Forked lightning crackled in clouds of ash. Falling ash stained and darkened the snow-bright slopes. In April the north face of the mountain started to bulge. The bulge grew five feet a day.

Sunday, May 18, dawned cool and bright. The sun edged higher in the sky, warming the air. The day promised to be beautiful.

Suddenly the promise was broken. At 8:32 A.M.

Clouds of ash and smoke rose miles into the sky, and drifted eastward, turning day into night.

the mountaintop exploded with a roar heard 300 miles away. Steam and hot gases blasted out of the north slope like the winds of a fiery hurricane. The mountain disappeared within a vast cloud of ash and black smoke. Huge chunks of ice and rock flew out of its side. An avalanche rumbled down the north slope.

The blast sent whole forests crashing to earth.

Clouds of ash spread eastward, cutting off daylight hundreds of miles away.

As heat melted ice and snow, water mixed with ash and ground-up rock, forming gigantic mudflows that were like wet concrete. The mudflows poured down the valleys, picking up boulders, trucks, and bulldozers, and carrying them along. They rushed into rivers, sending them over their banks. They ripped out steel bridges. They carried off logs, rocks, cars, and chunks of houses.

By nightfall only a small plume of steam rose from the volcano. The eruption was over. Some

The force of the blast snapped off and uprooted giant firs, scattering them like straws.

60 persons were dead or missing. Thousands of wild animals had died. More than 100 square miles of forest had been flattened. Valleys lay buried under mudflows. Ash blanketed everything for miles around.

The 1980 eruption of Mount St. Helens was the greatest explosion ever recorded in North America. Its violence surprised the earth scientists who had been studying the volcano since March. So did its suddenness, for most eruptions start

Mudflows engulfed some houses. Others were torn apart and carried off in pieces.

slowly. The scientists began searching for clues to why the volcano had blown up.

Like all volcanoes, Mount St. Helens is a place where hot rock from inside the earth moves to the surface. The rock is so hot that it is molten, and it has gases dissolved in it. The name for such rock is magma. Once the rock reaches the surface and loses its gases, it is called lava.

Mount St. Helens was built by lava. In some eruptions the magma was quite fluid and its gases escaped quietly. Lava flowed out of the volcano. In other eruptions the magma was thick and sticky. Its gases blasted out of the volcano, carrying lava skyward. You can see something similar happen with soda pop.

The liquid in soda pop has a gas — carbon dioxide — dissolved in it. When a bottle is opened, the gas starts to escape and makes bubbles. If you put your thumb over the top of the bottle and shake it, the gas expands. When you take your thumb off, you release the pressure. The gas shoots out of the bottle, carrying sprays of liquid with it.

The lava that was carried skyward from Mount St. Helens cooled into rock. Much of it was the kind of coarse, bubbly rock called pumice. Some-

times lava was blown apart into the tiny pieces of rock called ash. As this hardened rock rained down out of the sky it, too, built up the volcano.

Before the eruption of May 18, scientists expected Mount St. Helens to erupt as it had in the past. They knew that magma was moving inside the mountain. As it forced its way upward, it was tearing apart solid rock. The snapping of the rock caused earthquakes that made the mountain shudder. The bulge told them where the mountain was likely to give way. It seemed likely that magma would reach the surface at the place marked by the bulge and lava would erupt upward. Instead, something very different happened, as the scientists later discovered after months and months of studies.

The eruption, they found, was triggered by an earthquake, which shook the mountain. The shaking caused the whole gigantic bulge to break loose. The bulge slid away in the biggest landslide known in North America, taking with it a huge amount of rock ripped from the inside of the mountain. It was as if an enormous door had suddenly opened in the side of Mount St. Helens. The door faced not up, but sideways.

Until then, the inside of the volcano had been

something like a pressure cooker. In a pressure cooker, water is heated above its boiling point without turning into steam. As long as it is kept under pressure, it stays liquid. Inside Mount St. Helens, magma had heated groundwater, raising its temperature far above the boiling point. As long as the water was sealed in the mountain, it stayed liquid. But when the mountain was torn open, superheated water flashed into steam and expanded greatly. It exploded out of the volcano, breaking up rock, and carrying along fragments in its blast.

Late in the eruption some new lava did burst out of Mount St. Helens and turned to ash and pumice. But most of what came out was old rock. All told, three quarters of a cubic mile of old rock was ripped out of the mountain by the landslide and the eruption. By May 19 the peak of Mount St. Helens was about 1,200 feet lower than it had been on May 18.

As they discovered what had happened on the morning of May 18, scientists understood the suddenness of the eruption, which had taken them by surprise. But the eruption itself had not surprised them at all.

Mount St. Helens is a volcano that erupts fairly often. On the average it has erupted every 100 to 150 years over the past 4,500 years. Its last period of eruptions ended in 1857 — 123 years before the 1980 explosion.

Mount St. Helens is part of a chain of volcanoes in the Pacific Northwest. Together these volcanoes form the Cascade Range, which stretches from Lassen Peak in California to Mount Garibaldi in British Columbia. Mount St. Helens lies near

The Cascade Range is a chain of volcanoes that stretches from California to British Columbia.

the middle of the chain, in southern Washington.

Lassen erupted earlier in this century, and several other Cascade volcanoes have shown signs of life in recent years. Mount Shasta gives off steam. Mount Baker began stirring a few years ago. Mount Rainier is also very much alive.

The stirrings of these volcanoes do not surprise scientists either. The Cascade volcanoes are part of a still bigger group called the Ring of Fire.

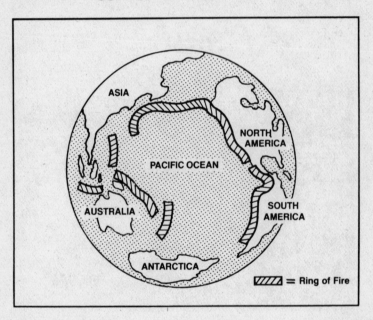

Ring of Fire is the name for the many volcanoes that rim the Pacific Ocean.

These volcanoes rim the Pacific Ocean, from South America to Alaska to Japan and Indonesia. Nearly three quarters of the world's active volcanoes are found in the Ring of Fire. Most of the others are in a belt of land that runs east-west between Indonesia and the Mediterranean Sea. In these same two regions most of the world's major earthquakes also take place.

A City Burns

Shortly after 5 A.M. on April 18, 1906, San Francisco was wrapped in the stillness of early morning. Here and there the quiet was broken by the clip-clop of a milkman's horse or the footsteps of a night worker heading home. The rest of the city was still asleep. Suddenly the sleepers were jolted awake as San Francisco shuddered in the grip of an earthquake. Around them bookcases and tall clocks tumbled. Pictures fell from walls. Chandeliers tinkled, swayed, and crashed to the floor.

People fled their houses. They snatched up pets, bowls, books — whatever came to hand —

and rushed into the streets in their nightclothes. The city shook a second and a third time. Chimneys collapsed. Sides were torn from houses. Streets were ripped apart.

Within minutes the earthquake was over, but the worst was yet to come — fire. When the city shook, wood and coal stoves overturned, spilling their glowing embers. Gas lines were torn open. Wisps and curls of smoke changed to crackling flames and clouds of black smoke. The fires spread,

After the earthquake of 1906, fires destroyed some 500 city blocks of San Francisco in two days.

until whole sections of the city were ablaze and the sky itself seemed to glow.

The fire department was short of water. The earthquake had shattered the mains that brought water into the city and carried it to hydrants. And so the fires burned for three days and two nights. By the afternoon of April 20, 500 city blocks had been gutted by fire and 28,000 buildings destroyed. Four hundred people had died in falling buildings or in fires.

The 1906 earthquake was not the first to strike

Outside the city, great cracks showed where the west side of the fault had jumped northward.

San Francisco, and it will not be the last. The city lies in a part of California where rock below the surface may suddenly shift or break, and when it does, the earth shakes.

Beneath its surface of oceans and soil, the earth has a layer of solid rock, which is called the crust. Most earthquakes take place because parts of the crust suddenly move. A few others occur because rock below the crust snaps or shifts. This rock is in the part of the earth called the mantle.

There are forces inside the earth that bend and

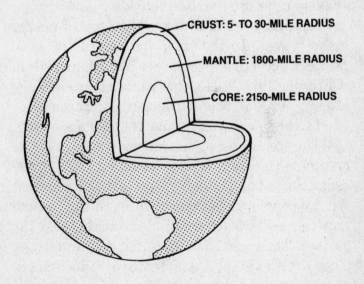

CRUST: 5- TO 30-MILE RADIUS

MANTLE: 1800-MILE RADIUS

CORE: 2150-MILE RADIUS

Interior of Earth

twist rock of the crust and upper mantle. They put the rock under great strain. When the strain becomes too great, the rock snaps.

You can see and feel the kind of thing that happens if you take a fairly thick stick and bend it. As you do, energy from your muscles is stored in the stick as strain. When you bend the stick past a certain point, it snaps, and the stored-up energy is suddenly released. The broken ends of the stick fly up, and you feel a sharp stinging in your hands. The stinging is something like the shaking caused by an earthquake.

The energy released takes the form of pushes called waves. In the stick one particle of wood pushes a second, which pushes a third, and so on. All through the stick some particles are pushing others. As the waves, or pushes, reach your hands, they push you — and you feel a stinging.

When rock snaps, a tremendous amount of energy is released. Waves shoot out in all directions. Some travel deep in the earth and are not felt by people. Some travel through the air and may cause a roaring sound. Some travel near the surface. These are the waves that do the damage. They are the ones that jolted San Francisco out of bed, knocked down buildings, and overturned stoves.

Once the crust has snapped, rock springs back into place. But a telltale crack remains. It is called a fault. Crust along the fault may remain quiet for years. The same forces however, are still at work within the earth, and they are bending and twisting the rock of the crust. In time the rock will snap again, probably along the same fault. And that is why the 1906 earthquake was neither the first nor the last for San Francisco. The city is near a big crack named the San Andreas Fault. It is millions of years old and more than 700 miles long. Seen from the air the fault looks like a giant puckered scar.

Seen from the air, parts of the San Andreas Fault look like a huge, puckered scar in the earth.

The earth has many other faults, places where the crust has broken. Some, like the San Andreas, appear as scars or valleys, but others cannot be seen because they lie too deep in the earth. Still others are hidden beneath the oceans. These are faults that run through the ocean floor. When rock along them snaps, a different kind of damage results.

In 1964, for example, Alaska was struck by a mighty earthquake. The earthquake waves were so strong that a mountain split apart and a whole peninsula moved 60 feet sideways, carrying along its mountains and lakes. A coastal region the size of Maine rose three to eight feet. In low-lying port towns, whole waterfronts slid into the sea. Highways buckled and railroad tracks were twisted into pretzels. In downtown Anchorage, automobiles bounced like balls and a 30-foot-deep hole swallowed a movie theater.

The earthquake lasted only about five minutes, but its damage did not end then. In that quake, rock snapped along an undersea fault in the Gulf of Alaska. The sudden movement created ocean waves of a special kind. Earth scientists call them tsunamis, a name that comes from the Japanese words for "harbor" and "wave." It is in harbors that these waves do their greatest damage.

In downtown Anchorage the shaking caused one side — but not the other — of this street to sink.

Tsunamis smashed harbors, casting boats ashore, carrying off buildings, then hurling them back.

Tsunamis get their start when an earthquake makes the ocean floor heave. The heaving creates a huge mound of water at the surface. The mound levels out into a series of broad, low waves. These waves are only two or three feet high, but they travel fast, at about 500 miles an hour.

As a tsunami nears land, it moves into shallow water. The front part of the wave is slowed, but the back part rushes on. It piles up on the front part, forming a giant wall of water. When this towering wave breaks, it crashes onto the shore and sweeps inland.

In 1964 port towns from southern Alaska to northern California were smashed by tsunamis. The waves crushed docks and waterfront buildings. When a wave drew back, it carried along houses, shops, boats, and fish canneries. Some of these were thrown back on shore by the next tsunami.

Hours after the earthquake ended, tsunamis thundered ashore in Hawaii. Traces of tsunamis were recorded thousands of miles away, in Japan and Antarctica.

That 1964 earthquake was one of the strongest ever recorded. Like the 1906 quake in San Francisco, it took place in the Ring of Fire.

For many years the Ring of Fire and the east-west belt were a scientific puzzle. Why did they exist? Did earthquakes and volcanoes occur in the same regions by chance? Or were they somehow related? Today earth scientists feel sure they know the answers to those questions. The answers are part of a strange story of oceans that open and close, of continents that drift across the face of the earth.

Southern Italy, part of the east-west belt, was hit by a severe earthquake in November, 1980.

Earth's rocky shell is broken into large plates.

Earth's Changing Face

Earth scientists have long known that the earth's rocky crust had cracks in it. But they used to think that the crust was all in one piece, like the skin of an apple. Today most believe that idea was wrong.

They now think the earth has an outer shell of rigid rock that is broken into big pieces, or plates. Each plate is about 60 miles thick. It is made of crust, and of rock from the upper mantle. The plates of rigid rock float on the very hot rock below. There are 10 or 12 big plates and some small ones.

The plates are in motion. They move very slowly, at an average rate of two or three inches a year, bumping and grinding against one another like chunks of river ice during a thaw. As they move, they carry along whatever is on top of them — the ocean floor, islands, and whole continents. Over millions and millions of years, the earth's land masses have drifted over the face of the earth, sometimes colliding and sometimes tearing apart. Where they tear apart, oceans open up.

Plate movement is so slow that we do not see it. But there are many signs of it, among them earthquakes and volcanic eruptions. Most of these take place along the boundaries of plates.

There are three kinds of boundaries: ones where plates drift apart; ones where plates collide; and ones where plates pass each other sideways.

Drifting Apart

Where plates drift apart, molten rock wells up from inside the earth, filling the space between them and forming new crust. The upwelling rock builds a ridge. Such a ridge runs down the middle of the Atlantic Ocean. It is part of a huge chain of ridges, or mountains, that runs along the bottom of every ocean, winding around the globe like the seam on a baseball. The chain is called the mid-ocean ridge. It is 40,000 miles long and hundreds of miles wide. Most of its peaks rise 1,000 to 10,000 feet above the ocean floor.

As molten rock wells up in the ridge, hardened rock is torn apart and swarms of earthquakes take place. Undersea volcanoes erupt, sometimes growing so tall that they become islands.

The mid-Atlantic ridge marks the place where, several hundred million years ago, the Americas

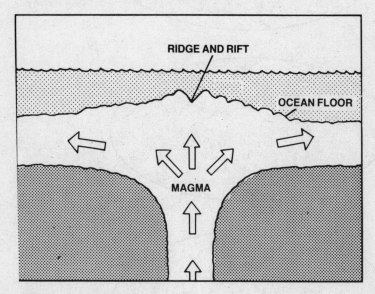

When plates drift apart.

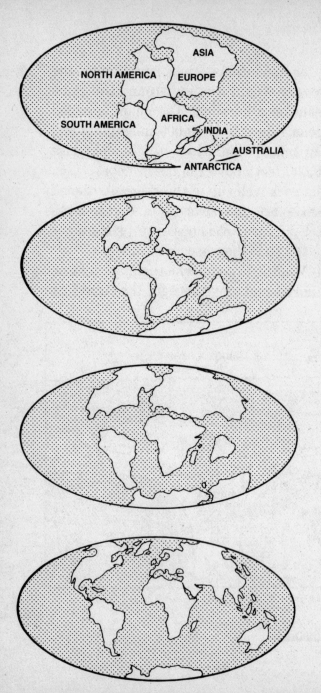

Earth scientists think that 200 million years ago there was just one big land mass, which they call Pangaea, surrounded by one big ocean. Rifts tore the land mass apart. In time the pieces became the continents that we know today.

were joined to Eurasia and Africa. At that time, earth scientists say, all the earth's land masses had collided. They formed one giant continent, which was surrounded by one big ocean. About 200 million years ago, a big rift opened under the supercontinent and tore it in two. Later, other rifts tore the two continents into smaller pieces. In time, they became the continents we know today. Riding the plates, they moved to where they are now.

As the Americas drifted westward on their plates, Eurasia and Africa drifted eastward. The

The jigsaw-puzzle fit of the Arabian Peninsula and Ethiopia and the Horn of Africa tells of the rift that has torn a large land mass in two.

gap between them filled with water. It grew into an ocean — the Atlantic. Because the continents are still drifting apart, the Atlantic Ocean is still growing wider. As it does the Pacific Ocean grows narrower.

Colliding

Around the rim of the Pacific, plates are colliding. When two plates collide, one of them slides beneath the other, into the mantle. That is why the Pacific is growing smaller — the Pacific plates are sliding into the mantle as other plates advance over them. It is also why earthquakes occur and volcanoes erupt around the rim of the Pacific. The sliding of plates puts rock under great strain. It snaps, and earthquakes take place. As plates slide into the mantle, rock melts, magma wells up, and volcanoes erupt.

For example, the plate under Alaska is colliding with the main Pacific plate. The big Pacific plate dives under it, pulling the ocean floor into a deep trench. Rock is put under great strain. When it snaps, an earthquake occurs. Where rock melts, volcanoes erupt.

The mid-ocean ridge swings close to the coast

of the Pacific Northwest. A small plate is drifting eastward from the ridge. It is in collision with the big plate carrying North America. The small plate dives under the big one. Rock melts and volcanoes erupt. That is how the Cascade Range formed and why Mount St. Helens erupts.

Sometimes two plates collide in mid-ocean. One slides under the other, forming an ocean trench. Beside the trench curved chains of islands are built up. They are made of lava that erupts from volcanoes. They are also made of rock and other materials scraped off the diving plate. The islands of Japan, Indonesia, and the Aleutians were all

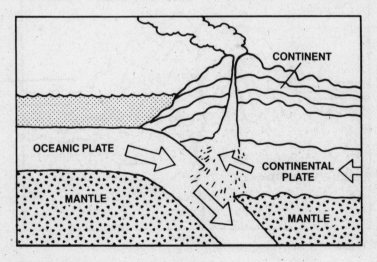

When oceanic and continent-carrying plates collide

formed this way. All have earthquakes and active volcanoes triggered by ongoing collisions of plates.

Sometimes two continent-carrying plates collide. They smash the land masses together and crumple the crust into mountains. The plate carrying India, for example, is in collision with the plate carrying China. The crumpling and buckling of the crust has formed the Himalaya Mountains. Earthquakes occur along the collision boundary and beyond, as the people of China have learned.

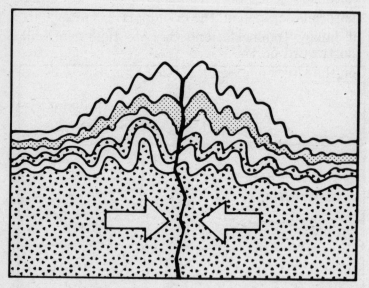

When two continent-carrying plates collide.

Passing Sideways

In the third kind of boundary, two plates move past each other sideways. The movement is not smooth. As giant slabs of rock move past each other, their edges grind together, snag, and lock. Strain builds up until the snagged rock snaps, and an earthquake takes place.

The San Andreas Fault is part of such a boundary. It marks a place where the main Pacific plate is moving northwest past the plate on which North America rides. For millions of years a long sliver of land west of the fault has been moving slowly northward on the Pacific plate. Towns and cities on the sliver are also moving. One of them is Los

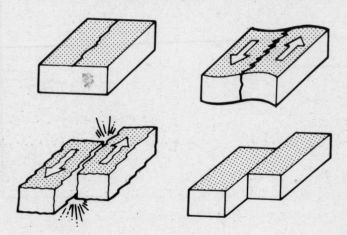

When plates move past each other.

Angeles, and in 10 million years it should be off the shores of San Francisco, which is on the east side of the fault. In about 60 million years, Los Angeles should be arriving at the Aleutian Islands.

It is strange to think of great plates drifting over the earth, colliding and jostling each other. Yet that is what most earth scientists think is happening. That is how they account for the fact that most of the world's big earthquakes and volcanic eruptions occur in the same regions — these are all plate boundaries. That is how they explain why, from time to time, the earth shakes and volcanoes erupt.

Some Famous Eruptions

Two thousand years ago, Vesuvius was a green and pleasant mountain where wealthy Romans built summer homes. The Romans knew the mountain was a volcano, but they thought it was dead. There was no record of its erupting.

· In the year 62, a violent earthquake rumbled through the region. It knocked down houses and heavily damaged the towns of Pompeii and Herculaneum. But no one even dreamed that it was caused by the stirring of Vesuvius. The houses and towns were rebuilt, bigger and better than ever.

In mid-August of the year 79, small earthquakes

Buried under 20 feet of ash from Vesuvius, Pompeii was discovered and dug out 1700 years later.

shook the region. The morning of August 24 dawned clear and bright. Farmers worked in their vineyards and orchards. In towns, bakers put bread in ovens and grocers set out their wares. Suddenly a violent earthquake struck, followed by a deafening crash of thunder. The top of Vesuvius split open and a huge cloud of glowing ash burst out of it. When the eruption ended, Pompeii was buried under 20 feet of ash that turned to cement in heavy rains. Herculaneum

Vesuvius is still a threat to towns and cities.

was buried by a mudflow 45 to 60 feet deep. When the towns were discovered some 1,700 years later, they were just as they had been when time stopped that August 24 — bread in the ovens, shops full of wares.

In the years that followed, Vesuvius erupted again and again. Then it fell silent for 600 years, until a big eruption in 1631. Towering above the Bay of Naples, the volcano remains a threat to this day.

In New England, 1816 was known as "the year without a summer." It began with normal winter weather, but soon people noted that spring was very late in coming. Frost killed crops in mid-May. In early June a five-day blast of wintry weather killed more crops. Snow fell in northern New England, and southern New England was gripped by icy winds and frost. Killing frost struck again in July and twice in August, destroying all but the hardiest crops.

The cause of the strange weather was a volcano that had erupted half a world away, in what is now Indonesia. On April 5, 1815, a volcanic mountain named Tambora began to destroy itself with blasts heard for 1,000 miles. For a week the mountain erupted, bathed in fire and blasting out huge volumes of ash, dust, cinder, and the bubbly lava called pumice. Hundreds of miles away mornings were as dark as night. Around the mountain itself whirlwinds tore down houses and ripped out large trees. Stones rained from the sky. The sea rose 12 feet and flooded island villages. By the time the eruption came to an end 4,000 feet had been blown off the top of the mountain and 10,000 people were dead.

The eruption sent a huge amount of fine dust into the atmosphere, where it stayed for several years. Circling the earth, the dust cut off sunlight. In many countries far from the volcano, temperatures dropped and crops were lost.

One of the strangest big eruptions took place in the same region, on the volcanic island of Krakatau.

In May of 1883 one of Krakatau's three cones began to rumble and give off puffs of ash. No one was alarmed. In fact, people from a neighboring island hired a steamer and visited the volcano. From time to time all summer the mountain continued to stir.

Around one o'clock in the afternoon of August 26 the island began to explode. Gigantic explosion followed gigantic explosion. By two o'clock a black cloud reached 17 miles into the sky. The explosions set huge waves in motion. By five o'clock the waves were battering the shores of neighboring islands, wiping out whole villages and plantations.

Just before 10 the next morning, the volcano fell silent. At two minutes past 10, the island blew up. A column of rock and fire blasted 50 miles into the air. When the eruption ended, most of the mountain had disappeared. Where had it gone?

At first people supposed it must have been blown to pieces — turned into dust and ash and small pieces of rock. But a strange discovery was made when samples of rock and ash were examined in a laboratory. They were not, as expected, old rock from the mountain. They were newly hardened lava. If it hadn't blown up, where had the mountain gone?

The answer was that it had sunk. Beneath the island there had been a shallow reservoir of magma. When the gas-filled molten rock all blasted out of the reservoir, it left an empty space. The mountain collapsed into the space and disappeared.

A very different kind of eruption took place on the island of Martinique in the West Indies. In the spring of 1902 the volcano named Mount Pelée began giving off puffs of steam, and rumblings were heard. All through April ash fell like snow on the city of St. Pierre at the foot of the mountain. It muffled the sound of carriage wheels in the streets. It drifted through open windows, coating furniture, floors, and draperies.

By early May the volcano was roaring and trembling. Ash falls grew heavier. Clouds of steam hid the top of the mountain. Some people left in alarm, but most did not because the government said there was no danger. It wanted everyone to stay for an important election.

The city of St. Pierre was destroyed by a superheated cloud of volcanic ash and gases in 1902.

At 7:52 on the morning of May 8, Mount Pelée erupted. There were three or four explosions. Then two black clouds shot out of the volcano. One rose straight into the air, blotting out daylight miles away. The other cloud, superheated and traveling at 100 miles an hour, swept down the mountainside and struck St. Pierre. Seeming to clutch the ground, it leveled the city with its blast and set fire to the ruins. It rushed into the harbor, sinking all but two of the ships waiting to take on cargo. Within minutes, 30,000 people died and the city was laid waste.

During the next several months similar clouds formed and were studied by scientists. They found that the people of St. Pierre had been killed by the blast of gases and the great heat of the cloud. They also discovered that each cloud had at its base a mass of red-hot broken rock. Each piece of rock was surrounded by an envelope of gas, and so there was almost no friction with the ground. Instead of being slowed, the red-hot rocks rushed along with the cloud. This kind of eruption is called a glowing avalanche.

Mount Pelée, like Krakatau and Tambora, was a big mountain known to be an active volcano. But sometimes a new volcano is born. Paricutín is a volcano that was born in a Mexican field.

On February 20, 1943, a farmer named Dionisio Polido went out to work his cornfield. He was startled to see smoke rising from one end of the field and terrified to discover that an 80-foot-long crack had opened in the earth during the night. Smoking gray-white stuff and red-hot stones were coming out of the crack.

Polido fled with his family to the village of Paricutín. Some of the village men went back to see what was happening. They found smoke, sparks, ash, and red-hot stones pouring from a pear-shaped hole in the ground. A sharp, unpleasant smell made them choke. Later they found a book at their church that told them what was happening: A volcano was being born.

By nightfall the volcano was roaring. Lightning flashed in the clouds of gas and ash pouring out of it. A cone-shaped hill was piling up around the opening in the ground. Two days later lava was flowing from a crack in the ground. It swallowed the Polido farm, the village of Paricutín, and another village. Ahead of it people and animals fled.

Meanwhile the volcano was growing rapidly.

Paricutín was born in a Mexican cornfield. Its lava destroyed two villages and covered the land.

During its first night it had grown 33 feet; it was 550 feet high by the end of the first week. Then its growth slowed, although lava continued to flow and ash to cover the countryside. The volcano was 1,345 feet high when, some nine years after its birth, it suddenly fell silent. It became one more of the quiet, cone-shaped mountains in that part of Mexico.

In late autumn of 1963 another new volcano was born. This one took shape on the floor of the Atlantic Ocean. It grew in an area where ancient eruptions along the mid-Atlantic ridge built the big island of Iceland and other smaller islands.

The chief sign of its coming was a bad smell that hung for two days over the Westmann Islands, off the southern coast of Iceland. It was the smell of rotten eggs — of sulfur. Search as they might, the islanders could not find where the smell was coming from.

Early on the third day the crew of a fishing boat noticed the same smell. By dawn they saw what looked like smoke rising from the sea. An undersea volcano was erupting. By that night on November 14, 1963, the top of a volcanic ridge had risen above the surface of the sea. And so the volcanic island named Surtsey was born.

By then nearly everyone realized what had been happening. Days or weeks earlier, a volcanic eruption had begun on the ocean floor. An underwater ridge took shape and grew. As its top neared the surface, gases bubbled up and into the air. They caused the sulfurous smell of rotten eggs. Columns of ash followed, looking at first like smoke.

By the morning of November 15, the top of the ridge was 33 feet above the water. Columns of smoke, gases, and steam billowed into the sky. Lava blasted into the air and rained down as ash and cinder. They built a cone that rose 500 feet above sea level by the time Surtsey was six weeks old.

Eruptions continued all through the winter. Storms and heavy seas attacked the loose material of the island. Parts of it were swept away. But the eruptions went on, and the material piled up faster than the sea washed it away.

In April lava began to flow. It covered the ash and cinder, forming a tough, hard surface. Lava reached the sea, cooled suddenly in the water, and built a collar around the new island. Waves still pounded the shore, but now they were pounding hardened lava. They could no longer eat away at the island, which went on growing until June,

Surtsey is a young island built by an undersea volcano. It first appeared in November, 1963.

1967. The new island of Surtsey had come to stay.

Most of the world's volcanoes erupt violently. They may erupt in different ways, but they are explosive. No one can study them close-up while they are erupting. But there are some volcanoes that erupt much more quietly, and these can be studied during eruptions. That is why the United States could build an observatory on an active volcano in Hawaii.

On the Edge
of the Crater

The Hawaiian Volcano Observatory sits beside the crater of Kilauea, one of the world's most active volcanoes. It has been there since 1912 and has never even come close to being blown up. The reason is that Kilauea does not erupt explosively, with great blasts of gases and molten rock. The volcano produces very hot, fluid lava. Usually the lava pours quietly out of long cracks, or fissures. The same thing is true of Hawaii's other two active volcanoes.

The scientists who study Kilauea are trying to

understand it and to predict its eruptions. One of their main tools is the seismograph, which records earthquakes and measures their strength. It can also be used to trace where they are happening. Earthquakes occur before nearly every eruption. But there can also be many earthquakes and no eruption, and so scientists need still other clues to find out what is going on.

A major clue may be the swelling of the volcano. Many volcanoes swell while filling with magma

A fountain of molten lava erupts from Kilauea.

and shrink when lava erupts out of them. The swelling can be detected with a tiltmeter.

Seismographs and tiltmeters provided clues to one of Kilauea's most dangerous eruptions. For two years the volcano had slumbered. In November, 1957, tiltmeters at the observatory hinted that the top of Kilauea was slowly swelling. At the time scientists had started to build tiltmeters that could be moved around as needed. Now the race was on: Could they get a network of tiltmeters in place before the eruption started? If so, they would learn a lot about the changes leading up to an eruption.

In October, 1958, seismographs began recording light earthquakes that went on into February, 1959. By spring the tiltmeters showed that the mountain was starting to bulge near a crater named Kilauea Iki. In August a swarm of small earthquakes occurred. Magma was moving in the mountain.

By November the network of tiltmeters was in place. They showed the mountain was filling with magma and swelling like a balloon. Shallow earthquakes were taking place at a rate of more than 1,000 a day. At 8:08 in the evening of November 14 the first eruption occurred. Cracks split open and fountains of red-hot lava gushed out of Kilauea

Iki. Lava poured into the crater, filling it to a depth of 335 feet. The eruption stopped, began again, and stopped. The lava ran back down its vent, like water going down the drain of a bathtub.

Between November 14 and December 21 Kilauea Iki erupted 16 times. Scientists seized the chance to collect gases and samples of lava. They measured the temperature and cooling rate of newly erupted lava.

The volcano fell silent, but the new tiltmeter network showed that the eruption was far from over. The mountain was even more bloated with magma than it had been at the beginning. Some-

A scientist takes a sample of red-hot lava on Kilauea, to study the nature of the molten rock.

thing was going to give way. A clue came in the form of a swarm of small earthquakes. Seismographs showed that the source of the quakes was moving eastward — fingers of magma were splitting rock. Observatory scientists tracked the earthquake to the village of Kapoho and a sugar plantation, some 30 miles from the crater. On the morning of January 13, 1960, the whole village began to shake. Trucks moved the people out.

Just after dark there was a great roar and a three-quarter-mile-long crack opened up outside the town. Lava fountains, some more than 300 feet high, danced in the dark sky. The eruption lasted 36 days and was one of the most severe Hawaii has ever known. The village and sugar plantation were buried under lava. But thanks to the warnings of tiltmeters and seismographs, no one was killed or even hurt.

In the years that followed, observatory scientists placed many more tiltmeters and seismographs around Kilauea. They studied changes in gases given off before eruptions. They looked for new kinds of clues that would help them predict eruptions. They came closer and closer to learning how to read Kilauea's changes. Then a strong undersea earthquake struck. It shook up the mountain and changed the pattern of eruptions. Scientists had to begin again.

The science of prediction is hard. No two volcanoes are quite alike, and even the same volcano may change its pattern.

Yet in a way, predicting earthquakes is even harder.

Lava flows down Mauna Loa in April, 1984 eruption.

The Question Is: When?

The San Andreas is a big fault. It comes ashore at the Gulf of California and runs north past Los Angeles and San Francisco to Cape Mendocino. There the fault goes back to sea. On land the fault is made up of a number of deep cracks that form a band. The band varies in width from a few hundred feet to a mile or more.

California has other fault systems where earthquakes also occur. But the San Andreas is the biggest and most important. It marks a boundary where plates meet and pass each other sideways.

There are places along the fault where movement is slow and fairly steady. Land west of the fault creeps north at perhaps an inch a year. Most of this creeping takes place in the middle part of the fault. Any visitor can see what is happening — where roads and fences cross the fault, they no longer line up. The parts on the west side of the fault have shifted north. In Hollister a warehouse that straddles the fault is slowly being torn

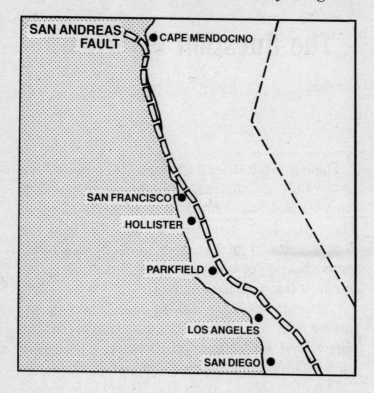

An earthquake struck California's San Fernando Valley in February, 1971. It shattered this freeway overpass, killed 64 people, and damaged or destroyed many buildings.

apart. Curbstones and ditches crumble where they cross the fault.

The slow creeping is not always smooth. Sometimes the edges of the plates lock together. Strain builds up and rock snaps, then the Hollister area is shaken by a small earthquake. But it has never had a big one. Before the strain becomes great, it is relieved by small earthquakes. This section of the fault does not worry earth scientists. As long as the slow creep continues, there will be no big earthquakes.

Other sections do worry them. These are the ones where there is no movement along the fault.

Plate movement buckles and bends rock formations, as this California highway cut clearly shows.

One section is near San Francisco. This part of the San Andreas Fault has not budged since 1906. At that time the fault shifted along a 250-mile-long section. North of San Francisco, at Tomales Bay, a road crossed the fault. When the earthquake ended, the road west of the fault had jumped 20 feet north. Since then the fault has been quiet and strain has been building up.

The other section is near Los Angeles. Areas around that city have had strong earthquakes in recent years. But they were caused by other faults. The San Andreas has not shifted since 1857. Then an earthquake struck at 8:33 on the morning of January 9, and it was one of the strongest in California's history. As the fault shifted along a 217-mile-long section, the ground shook violently for three minutes. Trees whipped back and forth, their branches touching the ground. Horses and cattle fell to their knees. A military post crumbled into ruins, and stream beds shifted as much as 30 feet. Even so, there was little loss of life or property. In 1857 few people had settled in southern California.

Today Los Angeles is the third biggest city in the United States. It is ringed by smaller cities and towns. San Francisco has also grown, as have its suburbs. In and near both cities are skyscrapers, dams, factories, power plants, houses, bridges, and highway overpasses. A really big earthquake would be a disaster.

At some time the long-quiet sections of the fault will move. That much is certain. The question is, when? It is a question that no one can answer yet. The same question faces scientists in other countries that have big earthquakes. All are looking for ways to predict when and where the earth will shake.

Over the years they have found many clues. In

In Japan — part of the Ring of Fire — schoolchildren learn in earthquake drills how to protect themselves.

some earthquake regions, the land tends to tilt. It slowly rises in one place and sinks in another. If the rate of tilting suddenly changes, a strong earthquake may occur. Other clues include changes in the level of water in wells, the release of gas from inside the earth, and changes in local gravity and magnetism. All are signs that changes are taking place inside the earth. Chinese scientists also report changes in animal behavior — cows breaking their halters to escape, chickens refusing to enter their coops, and rats staggering as if drunk. The problem is that the signs may foretell an earthquake — or they may not. China offers a good example of what can happen.

Parts of China have suffered many severe earthquakes, with great loss of life. Many Chinese live in houses made of mud bricks with tile roofs, houses that shake to pieces in earthquakes. But other kinds of building materials are scarce, and the people must make do with what they have. After a very bad quake in 1966, the government declared war on earthquakes. It built earthquake observatories. It built a network of stations to record small earthquakes, which often tell of big ones to come. It trained thousands of people to watch for changes that might tell of a coming quake, such as tilting ground and changes in water levels.

Over several years, the earthquake watchers found other clues. They noticed that ponds often became stirred up and muddy before an earthquake. So did irrigation canals. The ponds and canals might give off strange smells, perhaps of gases from inside the earth. Before big quakes the sky might glow with eerie flashes of light. Dogs would howl. Chickens flee their roosts. Rats and mice scurry out of houses. Fishes thrash about in ponds.

By 1974 Chinese scientists were studying Liaoning Province in Manchuria, where no strong earthquake had occured since 1856. Now a large part of the region had tilted and many small earthquakes were taking place. By December the scientists were predicting that a strong earthquake would take place within six months near the big port of Yingkow.

By late January wells were bubbling and animals were behaving strangely. Swarms of small earthquakes shook the region. A strange quiet followed.

On February 4, 1975, a decision was made. Three million people were ordered to leave their towns and cities. Quietly they put out their fires, closed their houses and shops, and moved outdoors to parks and fields.

At 7:36 that evening sheets of light filled the sky. The earth heaved and buckled. Roads crumbled, bridges fell, and farm buildings turned to dust. Cities looked as though they had been bombed. Without the warning tens of thousands of people would have died in collapsing buildings. As it was, only some 300 lost their lives.

Had the Chinese found a way to predict earthquakes? Earth scientists around the world hoped so. But their hopes soon faded.

In the summer of 1976 Chinese scientists thought they had found signs of a coming quake in Kwangtung Province. Again people were ordered to move into fields and parks. This time nothing happened. After two months of living in tents, the people were finally allowed to go home.

Chinese scientists had also been watching the area around Tangshan, a city in northern China. They had recorded some small earthquakes, some changes in gravity and magnetism. In late July water levels suddenly changed. Scattered reports of strange animal behavior were received. But the evidence of a coming earthquake was not strong. No warnings were given.

Just before four in the morning of July 28 the

earthquake struck. The sky blazed with light seen 200 miles away. The earth shook and heaved. Thousands and thousands of houses collapsed, and 20 square miles of the city were leveled. A big fault opened up in the center of Tangshan, tearing the walls off buildings and shifting parts of roads by four feet.

Other scientists have had the same things happen to them. Sometimes there are signs of an earthquake, and one occurs. Sometimes there are signs, but nothing happens. And sometimes there are few or no signs, and a quake strikes.

Much remains to be learned about predicting earthquakes and volcanic eruptions. But earth scientists have made great strides forward in understanding why most of the world's volcanoes and earthquakes occur in the same two regions. The theory that deals with plates has solved that puzzle. But the theory is not complete and there are still many other questions without answers. Some of them have to do with the volcanoes and earthquakes outside the Ring of Fire and east-west belt, with ones that do not occur along the boundaries of plates.

Hot Spots
and Other Puzzles

In the winter of 1811 – 12 three big earthquakes struck the southeastern tip of Missouri.

The first hit on December 16 at two o'clock in the morning. Around New Madrid, terrified settlers rushed outdoors as their cabins splintered. The night air reeked of sulfur, and the sky glowed with eerie flashes of light. Sections of forest were crashing to the ground. Huge cracks opened in the earth, and the Mississippi River became a raging sea of water.

The second big quake struck on January 23. The third, on February 7, was the strongest and most frightening of all. During that quake, land

Boatmen struggle as the 1811 earthquake turns the Mississippi River into a raging sea.

billowed, trees splintered, and a loud roaring filled the air. The Mississippi pulled away from its banks. It formed a mountain of water that crashed down and swept away boats and groves of trees. The heaving of the riverbed created two small waterfalls. Fields split open. Prairies became swamps. A whole lake was raised so high that its water drained away. The town of New Madrid was leveled. For hundreds of miles, from New Orleans to Boston, people felt that Missouri earthquake. It cracked plaster, stopped clocks,

Quake of 1886 left much of Charleston, S.C., in ruins and was felt as far away as Chicago.

and rattled windows in Richmond, Virginia. It rang church bells and broke up pavement in Washington, D.C.

The New Madrid earthquakes are a scientific puzzle, as are certain others. Among these are the big quake that struck Charleston, South Carolina, in 1886 and the smaller ones that rattle New England and eastern Canada. They do not fit into the general pattern of quakes. About 95 percent of all earthquakes take place where plates pull apart, collide, or grind past each other. But

Missouri, South Carolina, and New England are not on plate boundaries. They are not even near the edges of the North American plate.

Some volcanoes also occur within plates, instead of along boundaries where plates pull apart or collide. The island of Hawaii, for example, was built by five great undersea volcanoes. Three of them are still active. Yet Hawaii is in the middle of the big Pacific plate. How did it get there? Clues to the answer came from the ocean floor.

The Hawaiian Islands are part of a long chain of volcanic mountains in the Pacific Ocean. The chain stretches some 2,100 miles to the northwest, makes a sharp bend to the north, and then goes on for another 1,500 miles. Most of the mountains no longer rise above the ocean surface. Over millions of years they have been worn down by wind, rain, waves, and currents. No new material has been added to them because the volcanoes are dead.

The island of Hawaii lies near the southeast end of the chain and it has active volcanoes. Southeast of Hawaii a new volcano named Loihi is building up on the ocean floor and there are signs of a second new volcano nearby.

Earth scientists have dated the lavas in the chain of mountains. They found the youngest lavas in the southeast, where Hawaii is less than a million years old. The lavas grow older and older toward the northwest. At the far end of the chain they are between 42 and 70 million years old.

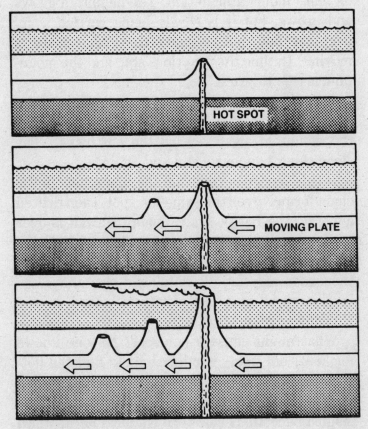

As a plate moves slowly over a hot spot, new volcanoes form and older ones are carried away.

These facts suggest that there is a hot spot beneath the Pacific plate, a place where a superhot plume of magma rises from the mantle. Its heat melts the crust. Lava erupts and over thousands of years builds a mountain. The mountain grows and grows, but it is slowly being carried away from the hot spot, because the Pacific plate is moving. In time the eruptions stop and the mountain ceases to grow.

The plume melts through another piece of plate. Lava builds a mountain. The moving plate carries the mountain away toward the northwest. The same thing happens again and again.

If this theory is right, all the mountains in the chain formed over the same hot spot, then drifted away on the Pacific plate. Today Hawaii is over or near the hot spot, but one day it, too, will drift away. Its volcanoes will stop erupting. In tens of thousands of years, Loihi should rise above sea level and become the youngest island in the Hawaiian group.

What might cause a hot spot? No one knows for sure, but many earth scientists find the hot-spot idea promising. It would account for volcanoes in the middle of plates. It might explain the magma beneath Yellowstone National Park, which heats the water of hot springs and geysers. It would also solve the puzzle of why Iceland exists.

That big island is part of the mid-ocean ridge. It is a place where floods of lava have built up the ridge and turned it into an island. The strange thing is that Iceland is the only island of its kind and size. The mid-ocean ridge is 40,000 miles long. But there is only one place where floods of lava have built a big island. It seems as if there should be more big islands or none at all.

A hot spot under Iceland would explain the floods of lava.

The earthquakes that take place within plates are much harder to explain. They occur along ancient faults. But no one knows how or when these faults formed. Nor does anyone know for sure what triggers movement along the faults.

Even so, earth scientists feel sure that most eruptions and earthquakes are signs of plate movement. They are equally sure that plate movement helps to make the earth a planet of life, and a planet that is home to many kinds of life.

A Planet of Life

Nearly three-quarters of the earth is covered by oceans. The continents rise above the water, giant islands in a big sea. The earth has been this way for hundreds of millions of years.

Yet land is constantly being worn away. Pounding waves and changing tides eat away the coasts. Whole mountains are worn down by scouring winds and rain, by fingers of frost and ice that pry off rock. Running streams carve channels in the land. Rivers carry soil and bits of rock into the oceans. It might seem that by now all the land should have worn away, that the whole earth should be covered by one big ocean. But this has not happened. The sea does not conquer the land. Continents and islands still rise above it.

The reason is that the earth stirs and the crust changes. It is worn down, but it is also rebuilt. Where plates collide, they force up strings of islands, thrust continents higher above the seas, or crumple new mountains out of the crust. Material scraped off a diving plate may be added to the edge of a continent, and the continent grows. Eruptions of lava add new crust. Thus the earth remains a planet of land and sea, a planet that can support life of land and sea.

It is not yet clear how the plates move — whether they are pushed, pulled, moved on the backs of currents in the mantle, or moved in some other way. But earth scientists do know what kind of energy drives them. The energy is heat, the earth's great inner heat.

The heat comes from certain kinds of atoms, such as those in uranium. These atoms are radioactive — they keep breaking down and giving off parts of themselves. The particles carry energy, which takes the form of heat. The amount of heat produced by radioactivity is small. But inside the earth billions of atoms are breaking down all the time, and little of their heat escapes through the earth's crust. Heat builds up inside the earth. Over millions and millions of years it becomes very great. It is great enough to drive huge plates of rock around the earth's surface. Along the boundaries, rock snaps and earthquakes occur. Volcanoes erupt.

A big volcanic eruption can wipe out a city, destroy an island, tear the top off a mountain. It can kill plant and animal life for miles around. Yet there are also ways in which volcanoes are helpful to life on earth.

The earth has had volcanoes since it was very young. Earth scientists suspect that volcanoes of the young earth gave us the air we breathe and the oceans. They think these formed from gases and steam released through eruptions. They think volcanoes go on adding to the air and oceans today.

Vast floods of lava have built land, such as Iceland and the Columbia River Plateau of the Pacific Northwest. Volcanoes have built islands such as the Hawaiian group. And on the new land, life has taken hold.

The island of Surtsey blasted its way out of the sea in November, 1963. Life of one kind or another soon began appearing on it. The island was only two weeks old when seagulls started lighting on

Eruptions of lava keep adding to Iceland, which is also being torn apart by spreading plates.

it between eruptions. By the following May the violent eruptions had stopped and lava was flowing, as it would for another three years. A biologist began looking for life on the island. He found migrating birds resting on it and microbes in the air. By summer there were butterflies and flies. Seals were hauling out on beaches. By the next summer, sea birds were nesting on newly built lava cliffs.

Seeds of shore plants, such as sea rocket and

lyme grass, drifted onto the island. So did some living plants. These first plants were soon buried under ash, but others took their place. Two years before the lava flows stopped, there was promise of the day when life would win a firm foothold on the new island.

Volcanic eruptions also help to make soil fertile by adding minerals that plants need. Some volcanic regions are among the most fertile in the world, and that is why people cluster in them — once an eruption ends, life does come back.

After the big 1980 explosion, parts of Mount

After the May 18 eruption, parts of Mount St. Helens seemed as gray and lifeless as the moon.

St. Helens looked like the surface of the moon — gray, silent, and lifeless. The forests of firs were gone. One huge area had turned into a plain of pumice. Valleys lay buried under hardened mudflows. Ash coated everything.

Yet within days of the eruption, the first signs of returning life appeared. Here and there, poking up through the ash, were green shoots of a hardy plant called fireweed. During summer and early fall, scientists found islands of plant life in the moonlike landscape. As well as fireweed, there were avalanche lilies, lupine, thimbleberry, thistles, asters. Their underground parts, such as roots and bulbs, had survived the eruption and sent up new shoots. There were also larger islands of life, meadows and groups of small trees that had been protected by several feet of spring snow at the time of the blast.

The survivors were joined by colonists. Seeds blew in. Where they could sprout and put down roots, new plants grew.

The plants made life possible for animals. Some were survivors — ants, pocket gophers, moles, deer mice — that had been underground at the time of the eruption. Some insects developed from eggs that had been underground. All were animals that either eat plants or eat animals that eat plants.

The animal survivors were also joined by colonists. Other insects flew or blew in and made their homes in the islands of life. Birds that find food in flowers or eat insects began to come back. Hummingbirds hovered at the flowers of fireweed and lilies. Juncos nested and laid eggs. Scientists saw robins, bluebirds, warblers, woodpeckers. They saw the footprints of coyotes, elk, deer, and squirrels, which had passed through looking for food.

Only three years after the blast, scientists counted 230 kinds of plants growing on the north side of the mountian. Herds of elk and deer were nearly back to normal. Scientists had known that life would come back to Mount St. Helens, but they were astonished at how quickly it was returning.

Life has always come back after the volcano's eruptions. Rain and melting snow mix ash into the soil, as do burrowing animals such as pocket gophers. Microbes put nitrogen in it. Rotting wood and needles and leaves enrich it. Seeds blow in, sprout, and take root. As more plants grow, more animals come to feed. Their hoofs and feet mix ash into the soil. Some bring more seeds in their coats or in their droppings. The new plants enable still other animals to come back.

One day nearly everything that used to live at Mount St. Helens will be living there again. The full return will take time, but it will happen. Volcanoes have long been part of our remarkable planet of life.

Three years after the eruption, school children and their teachers tour Mount St. Helens National Volcanic Monument.

INDEX